This is edition 1.
see p.19

About Tathāgata Zen

About Tathāgata Zen

•

JŌSHŪ SASAKI

Translated by Michel Mohr
Edited by Kendō Hal Roth

RINZAI•JI PRESS

Copyright 2014 © Jōshū Sasaki
ISBN 978-0-692-24335-0
All rights reserved. No part of this book may be reproduced, stored in a retrieval system or transmitted, in any form or by any means, without the prior written consent of the publisher.

RINZAI-JI PRESS
Rinzai-ji Zen Center
2505 Cimarron Street
Los Angeles, California
90018 United States
www.rinzaiji.org

EDITOR: Meg Taylor
DESIGNER: Counterpunch Inc. / Linda Gustafson
The calligraphy on the title page is by Jōshū Sasaki

PRINTED IN CANADA

Contents

About Tathāgata Zen   *Jōshū Sasaki*   7

NOTES   61
AFTERWORD   *Kendō Hal Roth*   67

「如来禅に就いて」
佐々木承周

　仏教と云う教えを始めて唱えたのは釈迦牟尼であると如来禅の修行者は伝承している。仏陀を一般に佛と略して日本では呼んでいるが覚者を意味して居るようである。では覚とは何を意味している状態であるかと云うに、日本では悟りと呼んでいるが、睡眠状態の自己が睡眠状態から目を醒ました状態を覚と云って居る。ですから、睡眠状態を覚とは云って居ないのである。覚に対して覚でない状態を迷と云って居る。では迷は睡眠の状態を指すのかと云うに、誰も睡眠の状態を迷の状態と云う人は居ないと想う。
　睡眠の状態が破れると人と呼ばれる存在者が生まれる。その人が聖人になったり、凡人になったりするのである。

About Tathāgata Zen

The practitioners of Tathāgata Zen have transmitted the idea that the first person to refer to "Buddha teachings"[1] was Śākyamuni. In Japan the word Butsu is generally used to refer to Buddha; Butsu translates literally as "awakened one." Now, what is the meaning of "awakening"—called Satori in Japanese? It refers to the state[2] in which the self, formerly asleep, "wakes up." Of course, one does not speak of awakening to describe the state of being asleep. To describe the unawakened state, we speak of delusion. Does it follow that delusion indicates the state of being asleep? I think that no one would confuse being asleep with delusion.[3]

When the state of being asleep dissipates, the existing entity called a person arises. This person sometimes becomes a saint, sometimes an ordinary being. For this reason, it

ですから、覚者が生まれる睡眠とはどんな睡眠かと見当されねばならなくなってきます。これは難しい問題であると云って可い。何れにせよ、仏陀とは悟った人のことを意味し、仏教とは悟った人の説かれた教えを捉えて居り、それが如来禅の立場である。従って誰でも良いから悟った人が現れて、その人が教えを垂れた場合、その人の教えが仏教と云うことになるのである。釈迦牟尼一人だけの教えを仏教と固定して呼んではいけない。それが如来禅の仏教の捉え方である。

　睡眠とは存在して居る物が取り上げる休息であるから、草木に至るまで取り上げて居る問題であると云ってよいでしょう。存在者つまり自己が睡眠と云う状態を現前して居る場合、睡眠の状態を離れて自己はないと考えて可いと想う。何故ならば睡眠の状態は、自己の全存在を云う全き状態を現前して居る状態と考えられるからである。最も自己が睡眠を現前して居ても夢を見ている場合もある。そう云う場合その自己は完全な睡眠と云う働きを現前していないと云って可い。何故ならば、睡眠の状態を静寂の状態と云うならば、その状態は静寂の現前とは云えないことになるからである。夢を見ると云うことは、やはり自己が何かをみることであって、何かを見る自己が現れなければ夢は成り立ちますまい。

is necessary to investigate which kind of sleep is the sleep from which an awakened being is born. Needless to say, this problem is rather difficult. The Tathāgata Zen approach is to understand Buddha as meaning an awakened person, and the Buddha teachings as the teachings given by such an awakened person. Accordingly, if an awakened person appears—whoever he or she may be—and this person delivers teachings, it follows that these teachings constitute Buddha teachings. Such a designation is not restricted to the teachings given by the individual called Śākyamuni. This is how Tathāgata Zen understands Buddha teachings.

Since sleep means that an existing entity is resting, one could say that this is a feature of all living things, including plants. When an existing person—namely, one's self—is manifesting[4] the condition called sleep, I think that we may consider that no self exists apart from the sleeping condition. Why is it so? Because it is possible to view the sleeping condition as the manifestation of a complete state involving the whole existence of the self. Obviously, while the self is manifesting the condition of being asleep it can also be experiencing dreams. In this case, we could say that the self is not manifesting the activity of perfect sleep. Why is it so? Because if we characterize the sleeping condition as total stillness, we need to admit that the dreaming condition does not manifest total stillness. After all, to speak of dreaming implies that the self is seeing something, and unless this seeing self appears, dreams cannot come into existence.[5]

また何かを見ようとする自己が現れてもその何かがない場合もあるでしょう。その場合夢を見ている自己は、無い何かを夢見て居るのである。全く夢である。また自己は何かに追いかけられて逃去る夢を見る場合もあるでしょうが、その場合自己を追いかけて居る者は何者であるかはっきりしない。然し何かが自己を追いかけて居る。それから自己は逃去るために、またそれを退けるために一生懸命になって逃げる夢を見る。然し何をしても、それから逃げることが出来ない。その間に自己は夢から目を醒ます。また求めるものが何であるか判っきりしないが、求める物に向かって走ったり飛んだりする。然し何をしても求められない。そのうちに目が醒める。

　こうした夢を幼年から少年の時代に渡って誰でもよく見たと想う。然し少し成長発達すると夢見る内容が変わってくる。今まで見たことのない女性の友の夢を見る。然もその女性に如何しても逢えない。自分の方を向いてくれればよいのだがと念願するが向いてくれない。そのうちに目を醒す。８０歳を過ぎると夢の内容がまた変わってくる。確かに夢を見たはずだが何を見ていたのか忘れてしまうのである。少年・青年・壮年・大人・老人の時に誰でも夢を見るでしょうが、夢を見ない時もあると想う。そう云う場合好く眠った、ああ清々しいと呼んで、新しい自己を捉えて目

We also need to consider the case when the self, wanting to see something, has appeared, but this something does not exist. In this case the self is dreaming about something inexistent: they are totally dreams. There is also the case when the self sees a dream in which he flees while being chased, but the identity of the person chasing him is unclear. Nevertheless, something is chasing him. Then, in order to escape, the self is dreaming about running away with all his might. In spite of this, the self cannot ever escape. The self then awakes while still in the midst of this pursuit. Sometimes, when it knows what it is seeking, the self runs or flies toward the thing being sought. It then wakes up while still doing this.

I believe that almost everyone experienced such dreams during childhood. Once we grow up and develop, the content of our dreams tends to change. We may see dreams involving a woman we have never seen before. Although it seems possible we might meet, we do not succeed in meeting her. Our dearest wish is that she look our way, but she does not turn toward us. And we wake up in the midst of this. Once we pass the age of eighty, the dreams change again. While still convinced we have had a dream, we tend to forget which kind of dream it was. Be it as a child, as a teenager, during the prime of one's life, as an older adult, or as an elderly person, everyone dreams. But there are also times that we don't dream. When this occurs we tend to say, "I slept well!" or "Oh, I feel refreshed!" as if we have woken up with a new self. Based on this type of experience we can all recognize the importance of the resting interval we call sleep. We may say that those

About Tathāgata Zen

を醒したような気を起こす。如何に睡眠という休息が大事であるかと云うことを、こうした経験から誰でも認めるであろう。新しい自己を現前したのであるという智を、毎朝捉え得る人は幸福な人であると言える。だからこうした経験をする人を蘇って現れた人と云っても、おかしくあるまい。

　如来禅修習者は好んで云う。禅を習うことは蘇りの自己現前を習うことであると。又必ず蘇るのであると教え示して居る。そのためには必ず夢を見ない本当の休息を取らねばならぬ。夢を見ない静寂を現前する練習を禅と云うのであると、禅者はまことらしく歌って居るようだ。確かにそうであるかも知れぬ。然し禅修習をしても静寂の自己が現れなかったらそれは禅ではないと云えるであろう。静寂の自己現前を可能にする禅であってこそ本当の禅であろう。然らば、寂静の自己現前を可能にする禅とはどんな禅か。

　作務と云う言葉で表詮した古人も居るが、動もまた禅と唱えた禅者も居る。要するに静に対する動であると云うのである。静と動とは対立する働きである。対立する働きが相互に関係しあって本当の禅が生まれるという意味であろうか。そうではないようである。静は動の結果として現れる世界で、意思意欲を失って現れる働きを内容として現れる世界である。それが静の体である。動は相対立する働きが

who can recognize the wisdom of having manifested a new self every morning are happy. Thus, it wouldn't be excessive to state that those who have had such an experience are people who appear to have been reborn, or one could even say, resurrected.[6]

Students of Tathāgata Zen are fond of saying that the study of Zen entails learning to manifest a reborn self. They also teach that without fail one comes back to life. For this to occur, it is imperative to truly rest without dreams. On the other hand, some Zen practitioners claim in good faith that this type of learning and practice, manifesting total stillness is what is called Zen. It cannot be denied that this claim may contain some truth. If one studies and learns Zen without manifesting the self of total stillness it cannot be called Zen. Proper Zen occurs only when it makes the manifestation of the self of total stillness possible. In that case, which type of Zen is the one that makes the manifestation of the self of total stillness possible?

Some ancients posited[8] that manual labor (*samu*) was an approximation, while others claimed that movement was Zen. Essentially, they described stillness as opposed to movement. These two aspects called stillness and movement represent opposite activities.[9] By saying that they represent opposite activities, does it mean that it is within their mutual relation that true Zen is born? It does not seem to be the case. Stillness is a world that emerges as the result of movement, and the content of this world emerges when both desire and will have disappeared. This constitutes the essence of stillness. Movement

一体の状態を現前したり、分離の状態を現前する働きである。相対立する働きが一体を現前した状態が静である。だから静は動の結果として現れる体であると云うのである。

相対立する働きが一体を現前したり、逆に一体になった体が分離するという話は、難しい話だと云ってよい。何故ならそれは矛盾した働きを現前していることになるから難しい。然し意思のない対立の働きならば今日の人は容易に理解することも出来よう。つまり「＋」と「－」が一緒になれば零になると云うことは誰にでも理解出来ることであるからである。然し逆に零が二つに分離すると「＋」と「－」になるという理解は一寸出来にくいだろう。何故ならば一般の人は直ちに零の当体をナイフを以て二つに分けることを考えるからである。然し零は他の力を借りて二つに分かれるのではない。自力というか自然の働きとして分離するのであると云われたならば、直ちに自分は零になって自分を二分するであろう。つまり「＋」と「－」である。つまり自分を有と無との対立した働きに分離するであろう。或は生と死との働きに零を容易に分けるであろう。

然るに自己は生きる働きをせねばならぬ者として存在し

is what occurs after we manifest the condition in which these mutually opposing activities have become unified; this is the activity that manifests the condition of separation. Stillness is the condition that manifests when the mutually opposite activities have become one. Thus, one can say that stillness is the essence that appears as the result of movement.

This discussion about how mutually opposite activities may become one, or conversely how this unity separates, is rather difficult. Why is it so? It is difficult because it deals with the manifestation of activities that are paradoxical.[10] Yet it should be easily understandable if it were described as the activity of an opposition devoid of intention or desire. In other words, it is because everyone can understand if one explains that when "plus" and "minus" come together the result is zero. On the other hand, it is hard to follow the opposite reasoning, saying that when zero splits into two it results in "plus" and "minus." Why is it so? Because most people instantly think of cutting the very essence[11] of zero into two pieces with a knife. Yet zero does not separate into two pieces by borrowing some external power. Whether or not it is labeled "self power," this entity (*jibun*)[12] becomes zero in an instant and divides itself into two as a result of its spontaneous activity. Namely, it is both plus and minus. In other words, it separates itself into two opposite activities: being (*u*) and nonbeing (*mu*). Alternatively, it may be easier to understand if we say that zero separates into the two activities of life and death.

For all that, when we envision this from the perspective of the functioning of consciousness,[13] the idea that the self exists

て居るのであると云う考え、つまり意識作用の上に立って居る場合、その自己は死の働きと一体となって零すなわち静寂の状態を現前することは、とてもとても、難しい問題である。むしろ出来ないと云うことになるであろう。然し自己が意思意欲のない働きをして居るその者が自己であると気が付いた場合、自己は死の働きと容易に関係を結んで一体を現前するであろう。死の働きを退けることが無くなるのである。誠に自己は何をせばならぬとか、生きる働きをせねばならぬとか云うように意思意欲を持った自己になると、他と関係を結ぶことが困難になってくる。自己と云うものを肯定してくれる者とは進んで関係を結ぶが、自己を否定するものに出会うと自己はそれを退けるのである。

　静寂を現前する修習を前に禅と云うったが、禅とは何であるか、これで少し理解が出来たと云えるのでよいかと思う。禅とは不完全な意識作用を自己とする、そうした自己を否定して、完全な意識作用を現前する自己とすることを修習する働きの現前であると、禅修習者は知るであろう。然も動の働きの結果が静であって意思意欲のない働きであって、その静は完全知を現前して居る智であると云うことを禅修習者は頷くであろう。

　然らば不完全智を自己とする自己はどこから生まれてく

as a person who must perform the activity of living makes it extremely difficult to conceive of the fact that this self becomes one with the activity of death; namely, that it manifests zero or the condition of absolute stillness. One could say that it appears impossible. Yet once the self becomes aware that the person whose activity is devoid of will or desire is the true self, this self can easily establish a relation with the activity of death and manifest oneness with it. Our rejection of the activity of death disappears. In contrast, if you ask, "What should the self do?" or tell yourself, "I must perform the activity of living," then it becomes difficult to establish sincere relations with others. The self is keen to establish relations with those who affirm its existence, but when it encounters people who negate its existence, then the self rejects them.[14]

We have mentioned that the learning and practice that manifest total stillness can be called Zen, but what is Zen? Since you have gained some understanding through this explanation, I think that it should be fairly clear. Zen practitioners should know that Zen is the manifestation of an activity negating the self built on an incomplete functioning consciousness, and cultivating the self manifesting a complete functioning consciousness.[15] Additionally, Zen practitioners may nod in agreement when told that the result of the activity of movement is stillness, an activity without will or desire, and that this stillness is a cognitive acuity[16] manifesting complete wisdom.[17]

On the other hand, the self that considers incomplete wisdom as itself, where does it emerge from? It is because this

About Tathāgata Zen   17

るのか、そうした自己が生まれてくるから完全自己の現前を習うのであるが、不完全自己は何処から来るのか。それは零が二つに分かれた場合に現れるのである。こうしたことは最っと微細に調べなければ分かりにくい問題であるが、先ず禅とは何であるか心する必要があるため述べたのである。

　相対立する働きを大別すれば、生と死・善と悪・膨張と収縮、存在すると云う働きと存在しないと云う働き・有と無・光明と暗黒と云う風に対立の働きを沢山挙げることが出来る。しかし研究の都合上、生とか膨張とか有とかと云う風に肯定する働きを実と命名し、死とか収縮とか無とかと云う風に否定する働きを賓と命名して留まることなく更に修行することにして居るのが如来禅の立場である。相対図する二つの働きを内容として、この宇宙万物を宇宙の内に顕現すると共に、逆に顕現した存在者を隠滅の世界に即ち宇宙は導き容れる働きをしておると、前代未聞と云ってよい考えを現前するように、若い時代のゴータマ悉達多（シッタルター）は成長発達したと如来禅修習者は伝承しておるのである。然もこの無常の働きは積極的に賓が活動して賓主分離を展開し、次に賓主一体を現前して動かざる星・沈黙の星・北極星まで拡大し、そこを限度として止ま

incomplete self has been born that one has to learn how to manifest the complete self, but where does this incomplete self come from? It appears when zero has split into two. This issue is difficult to understand unless one investigates it in the most meticulous way; but since an understanding of this issue is necessary to answer the question "What is Zen?" I will discuss it first.

In order to roughly distinguish groups of mutually opposing activities, one could list many examples such as life and death, good and evil, expansion and contraction, or the activity of existence versus the activity of nonexistence, being and nonbeing, or light and darkness. Yet, for the sake of investigating these various facets and ceaselessly refining ourselves,[18] the Tathāgata Zen approach designates as "reality" all positive modes of activity such as life, expansion, and being, whereas it designates as "guest" the opposite modes such as death, contraction, and nonbeing.[19] The content of this scheme illustrating the two opposite activities reveals how all phenomena in the universe manifest in its fold; on the other hand, it also shows how the universe performs the activity of inducing existing entities toward the realm of obliteration.[20]

The practitioners of Tathāgata Zen have handed down the idea that the young Gautama Siddhārtha actualized this vision—which had hitherto been unheard-of. Moreover, he implicitly recognized[21] that the activity of impermanence, through the movement of the progressively increasing guest, develops into the separation between guest and host.[22] Next, this movement manifests the unification of guest and host,

About Tathāgata Zen   19

るものであると暗々裡に承知していたと伝承されておる。そればかりでなく、そこから逆に主の働きが起こって根源の立場に座り、それが無常の働きであると深く考え込んでDhyānaの修習に熱中したと伝承されて居る。

　つまりゴータマ悉達多は若い時代に色々な学者や遊行僧に就いて学問をしたと伝えられて居る。ですから当時の印度における学者の世界観や人生観、それから国家が必要とする政治家や天文学者に学んだに相違ない。つまり当時の印度は釈迦牟尼と云う聖者を世に出す準備の国としての文化を咲かせていたのである。如何に釈迦牟尼が超人的な偉人であっても、意思意欲なき空の働きが一切を造作し逆に一切を滅に導こうと云う哲理を独創したに相違ないが、その準備は先哲の偉人達に依って成されていたと見るべきであろう。

　つまり古代の印度人に依ってカルマと云う働きが発見されて居る。そうしたカルマは何人も何物も逃れることは出来ないと云う思想を古代の印度人は生み出して居るのである。だからカルマは絶対的な働きを云うことになるであろう。ところが人智が進歩して色々な神が印度に現れるようになる。遂にブラウマンが現れて一切創造の座に座る人格神として仰がれるようになる。だからカルマをこの

expanding as far as motionless stars, silent stars, and the North Star, which were regarded as the limit. It was also taught that Gautama Siddhārtha became absorbed in the practice of *dhyāna* while thinking deeply about how, conversely, the activity of the host occurs through its being anchored in the standpoint of the source (*kongen no tachiba*),[23] and how this also constitutes the activity of impermanence.

In other words, it tells us how during his youth Gautama Siddhārtha deepened his learning by studying with all sorts of contemporary Indian scholars and itinerant monks. We can assume that he studied the worldview and the different approaches to human life held by learned scholars but also by politicians and astronomers. In those days India possessed a flourishing culture, which made this land fit for the emergence of the sage later known as Śākyamuni. No matter how exceptional Śākyamuni was, even in his undeniable creation of the philosophical principle according to which the activity of emptiness devoid of will and desire produces everything and, conversely, induces everything toward annihilation,[24] we should consider that the preparation for this was done by relying on the exceptional sages who preceded him.

The activity of karma had already been discovered by the ancient Indians. They developed the idea that nobody and nothing can escape the law of karma. This is why it can be said that karma represents an absolute activity. Human wisdom advanced, and various divinities started to appear on Indian soil. Eventually, Brahman was revered as a divinity with human features. Brahman occupied the central

人各神は司宰することになる。我々人間の前に万物の人格神が現れると云うことは、人間にとって幸福なことだと云ってよい。然しその万能者は完全に人間を救ってくれるのであろうか？自己の求めるものに就いても退けるものに就いても完全に保護してはくれないと云ってよい。

　人格神は人間のように生を愛し死を憎んで居るように見える。それではカルマを司宰する神ではなかろう。万能者は生の働きも死の働きも内容として存在して居る者でなければなるまい。退けるものがあっては万物者ではない。前に云ったように自己は生の働きをしなければならぬものとして存在して居るという場合、その自己は死を退けて居るのである。つまり一切を形成する生と死と云う対立の働きを退けて居る自己なのである。だからその自己は片輪の自己であって本当の自己でない。即ち不完全な意識作用をして居る。意識作用を自己として居る自己なのである。そう云う自己をアートマンと捉えておるのが仏陀であると如来禅では伝承して居るのである。

　つまり漢訳で支那の仏者の云う我であって片輪の自己を指して云って居るのである。そう云う風に一方の働きに偏して自己を現前して自己を主張する場合、その主張を我見と云って居る。そういう我の自己は不完全な意識

position of the Creator. It was understood that this divinity with human features presided over karma. We could say that when this divinity with human features, having created everything, appeared in front of us human beings, it was a blessing. But will this omnipotent being provide humanity with complete salvation? It is reasonable to say that regarding what the self wants and regarding what the self would like to avoid, no deity will provide a complete guarantee of salvation.

It appears that a divinity with human features is attached to life and hates death, like human beings. In that case, this deity cannot preside over karma. An omnipotent being should be a being whose existence encompasses both the activity of life and the activity of death. If there is anything that it tries to avoid, then this is no omnipotent being. As mentioned above, as long as the self exists as a being who must perform the activity of living, this self is avoiding death. Namely, it is a self who is avoiding the opposite activities of life and death, which are shaping everything. It means that this self is one-sided and not the true self.[25] That is to say, it is a consciousness that is functioning incompletely. It is a self that considers incomplete consciousness as its true self. Tathāgata Zen has handed down the idea that the one who apprehended this self and designated it as the *ātman* was the Buddha.

- In China, Buddhist translators used the word "I" (*wo* in Chinese; *ga* in Japanese) to indicate this one-sided self. In this way, when it is manifested as a self biased toward only one type of activity and asserts itself, this self-assertion is what we call self-centeredness. Because this self-centered self con-

About Tathāgata Zen   23

作用を我として居るから自己が何処に存在して居るか分からない、即ち自己を取り逃がして居るのである。自己は云うなれば後に説き示すように、外側に位いする「賓」即ち生の働きと内側に眺られる「主」即ち死の働きに包容されて存在しているのである。だから我の自己の立場に戻って外側の「賓」に包容され、内側の「主」に包容されて居るという考えを起こせ！と如来禅では教え示して居るのである。自己が我の立場を解消して本来の立場に立つと、不完全の自己を解消したのであるから、本当の自己の立場に不完全の自己が立つことになる、よって住居場所を禅学としなくなる。然るに不完全な自己の立場に立つと、光輝く片輪のブラウマンに外側から、暗黒の片輪のブラウンマンに内側から包容されて居る不完全な智を発揮するようになる。それでは、カルマの働きからも、ブラウマンからも自己は自由な立場になれまい。自由な立場で真実な自己とは内と外側とに位する「賓」と「主」を共に内容とする自己が現れた場合で、ブラウマンからもカルマからも自由になるのである。

　斯したカルマを無常の働きとして仏陀は悉達多の時代に既に捉えていたと云うのである。然しながら悉達多はアートマンを解消して本来の自己の立場に帰らねばなら

siders the incomplete consciousness as "I," it does not understand where the true self exists; this self evades its grasp. As explained below the self includes both the guest or "servant" on the outside, which corresponds to the activity of life, and the host or "master" on the inside, which is the activity of death. Thus it is taught in Tathāgata Zen: return to the standpoint of the "I am" self and produce the awareness that you are enveloped by the guest outside and by the host inside! When the self dissolves the "I am" perspective and takes its original standpoint, because it has dissolved the incomplete self, the incomplete self is now standing in the position of the original self and its abode has disappeared as an object of Zen study-examination. However, standing in the position of the incomplete self, because it is enveloped by the luminous one-sided Brahman on the outside and the darkened one-sided Brahman on the inside, the situation of incomplete wisdom is evident. Since this is the case, because of both the activity of karma and Brahman, the self will not become free. Freedom is attained by the true self when that self manifests the condition in which the host inside and the guest outside are its content; it will then become free from both karma and Brahman.

It is said that when the Buddha was still Siddhārtha he identified this function of karma as the activity of impermanence. Although Siddhārtha had obtained the wisdom according to which one must return to the standpoint of the original self (*honrai no jiko*)[26] after having eliminated attachment to the ātman, he still could not attain the wisdom that would allow him to teach people a way to understand the activity of

About Tathāgata Zen   25

ぬと云う智を得たが、無常の働きの理を人にも解るように説き示す智を有つ事が出来なかった。然し無常の働きの外にどんな真理もないと確信したのである。だから無常の理を説き示す智を如何しても克ち取らねばならぬと苦心したと云うのである。

　信念に燃えれば燃える程信念は強化される。その信念を正しい理と説き示す智が沸き出してこない場合それ程苦しいことは無かろう。悉達多はそうした苦悩に出会ったのである。自分は自己の信念を説き示す智を如何して克ち得ることができないのか。現に生きて居る自己が本当に死に出会う経験をしてないからである。自分は妻子の愛情にも恵まれ、又恵まれた生活をして居る。だから愛情の否定にも出会う事はなく、貧の生活に出会う事もない。そのため自己は無常の働きを知る真知を克ち得ることが出来ないのであると考えたと云うのである。如何しても無常の働きに出会う経験をせねばならぬと決意したと云うのである。そこで沙門になることを決意したと云うのである。もっともこれだけの理由で沙門になったのではなかろう。最っと最っと理由のあったことと思う。とにかく沙門となって前後６年間の修行をして無常の働きを説き示す智を克ち得たと伝承して居るのが如来禅の立場である。

impermanence. Yet he was convinced that there is no truth aside from the activity of impermanence. This is why he made strenuous efforts to attain[27] the wisdom that would allow him to teach the law of impermanence.

The more someone is burning with a strong belief, the more that belief gets reinforced. There is nothing as excruciating as when this belief consists in the wish to obtain the wisdom to explain a certain law and this wisdom does not even begin to emerge. Siddhārtha experienced such agony. He was wondering why he could not obtain the wisdom to explain a certain law that he personally believed. This was because the self who was currently living had not experienced truly running into death. He was blessed with the affection of a wife and a child, and was also leading a blessed life. Thus, he had never run into the negation of affection, and never run into a destitute life. It is told that he thought this was the reason why his self could not obtain the true wisdom to understand the activity of impermanence. Accordingly, he made the resolution that through whatever means, he had to experience the activity of impermanence. It is told that this is how he decided to become an itinerant monk.[28] Be that as it may, he probably would not have become an itinerant monk only for this reason. I think that he must have had a much stronger reason. In any case, the Tathāgata Zen approach has handed down the narrative that he became an itinerant monk, and after having spent approximately six years absorbed in practice, he achieved the wisdom to explain the activity of impermanence.

仏教には五蘊と云う教えがある。それは仏教の趣旨を説き示して居る根本の教えとして如来禅では取り上げて居る。仏教とは悟った人の教えであるが、一般に仏教と云う場合仏陀の教えを仏教と云って居る。その仏教の創始者である釈迦牟尼が入滅されてから、発展的な教派が生まれた。そう云う教派の五蘊の説明と如来禅が説き示す解説は必ずしも同じではないということを断って置く。何となれば如来禅では五蘊の教えと人生観の問題と世界観との問題を、釈迦牟尼が説き示して下された教えとして受け取っているからである。

　つまり五蘊の教えを秘訣として伝授して居るのである。しかし他の教派の批判を怖れて秘訣としてきたのか何か解らんが、今日では秘訣として置く必要はない。学者方の批判を仰いで発達されるべきと考えたのである。それで秘すことなく述べるべきである。然し聞きなれない人に取っては（仏教の話は難しい点が相当に現れる）難しく感ずる点が現れる。その場合自説（I am）を入れるので却って解らなくして居るかも知れない。　注意して学んで貰いたい。

　五蘊とは五つの蘊と云うことである。識蘊、行蘊、想蘊、

VIJNANA = cociousness

BODHCITTA = VOLITIONAL FORMATION

The Buddha teachings include a teaching called the five aggregates, or *skandhas*.²⁹ In Tathāgata Zen this is considered one of the fundamental teachings. Although the Buddha teachings are the teachings of an awakened person, what people generally mean when they use the word *bukkyō* is Buddhism as taught by the Buddha. After Śākyamuni—the founder of Buddhism—passed away, numerous traditions unfolded.³⁰ I must warn that the explanation of the five aggregates given by these traditions is not necessarily identical to the interpretation provided by Tathāgata Zen. The reason for this is that in Tathāgata Zen the teaching of the five aggregates, how one envisions human life, and one's worldview are all understood as teachings revealed by Śākyamuni.

The teaching of the five aggregates was imparted from teacher to disciple in Tathāgata Zen. Whether it was treated as a secret teaching³¹ out of concern that other traditions might criticize it, I don't know, but today it is openly discussed. I think that this should be further advanced through exposure to criticism from scholars. It must be stated clearly, without hiding anything. Nevertheless, there are elements that those unused to such terminology will find difficult to grasp—so many difficult elements arise when speaking of the Buddha teachings. In this case, the difficulty in understanding may increase because the teachings are generally envisioned from the perspective of the first person ("I am"). Please study closely what follows.

The five aggregates indicate five *skandhas* or bundles: the *skandha* of consciousness, the *skandha* of volitional forma-

About Tathāgata Zen   29

受蘊、色蘊の五つを云うのである。蘊とは梵語でスカンダと呼ばれて居る。この蘊の思想は古来から刹帝利つまり貴族階級に伝った思想というか教理というか、とにかくそういう考えであると伝承されて居る。然るに蘊とはタバネルことを意味するが、名詞に用いられたりまた動詞に用いられたりして居る様である。又心の働きが乱れて居る場合に、一点に統一する働きの意味にも用いられて居る。ところが如来禅で散乱して居る物を把住（包容）したならば、逆に散乱しなければならぬ、散乱した状態があって蘊と云う働きもできるのであるから、その逆の修習をせねばなぬと強調し逆の蘊の意味の修習を表す言葉と捉えて居る。それは実習を強調するから如来禅ではそう捉えて居るのであって、他の教派では取り上げていない解説だと思う。

　つまり蘊はそれ自身で散乱して居る状態を一点に集中し、一点に集中した状態を逆に散乱する働きを蘊と云うのであると如来禅では取り上げておるのである。ですから蘊と云う働きは如来禅でいう禅の働きと同じであると云ってよいのである。然し蘊は刹帝利と云はれる貴族階級に伝わって伝えられて居る教えであるとすれば、

tions, the *skandha* of perception, the *skandha* of sensation, and the *skandha* of form.³² The Chinese character pronounced *un* in Japanese corresponds to *skandha* in Sanskrit. It has been handed down that this school of thought or doctrine revolving around the *skandhas* was transmitted among the members of the Kṣatriya or warrior class in ancient India, who constituted the ruling nobility. The Chinese character *un* means "to bundle up"³³ and it seems to have been used either as a noun or as a verb. Further, when the activity of the mind is chaotic,³⁴ "bundling" can also be used to mean the activity of unifying the mind to a single point. That is, in Tathāgatha Zen, if one fully embraces³⁵ the thing that is scattering, the opposite of scattering must be happening. Because when the mind is scattered the activity of "bundling" is possible, learning to practice³⁶ the opposite activity must also be done; this implies learning to practice unification, the opposite of the commonly held meaning of "a bundle." This is how it is understood in Tathāgata Zen, which emphasizes practical learning,³⁷ but I don't think that other traditions mention this explanation.

In other words, Tathāgata Zen considers that the *skandhas* concentrate their own scattered condition in one point and, conversely, that the *skandhas* also mean the activity of scattering this condition of single-pointed concentration. This is why one could say that the activity of the *skandhas* is identical to how Tathāgata Zen envisions the activity known as Zen. Yet if we assume that the *skandhas* result from a teaching transmitted among the Kṣatriyas or members of the nobility—because it implies that this teaching was only necessary to the

About Tathāgata Zen   31

貴族階級のみが必要とした教えであるということになるから、Dhyānaよりは、はるかに新しく生まれた言葉であると云えるだろう。

　Dhyānaはアーリヤ人が亡ぼしたのでないかと言われて居る先住民族が残した精神的文化財でよいかと云われて居る。それを証明して居るが如しDhyānaは奴隷階級に至るまで修習して居る、独特の精神修養の宗法である。Dhyānaは静慮と意訳されて居る言葉で、乱れて居る心の状態と一点に集中にすることを云うのであるが、またその修習をもDhyānaと言うて居る。

　このDhyānaも心の乱れて居る状態を一点に集中する修練だけでは自己と云うものを完全に仕上げる修練にはならない。それでは偏った修養方法と云う事になる。何故なら、心の乱れる働きを束縛することになる。心が乱れると云う事も心の働きなのであるから、心の乱れる働きを即ち心の散漫する働きをも修習せねばならぬ。即ち一点に集中した心の状態を逆に散ずると云う働きをせねばならぬ。そう云う修習をしてこそ心の働きの全体を修習することになる。これが本当のDhyānaと云うことにならねばならぬとし、本来のDhyānaを単なるDhyānaと呼び如来如去の禅即ち略して如来禅と唱えたのである。

noble class—we can assume that the word *skandha* emerged much more recently than the word *dhyāna*.

The word *dhyāna* can be regarded as the spiritual legacy of the Aryans, the aboriginal people of India who have disappeared.[38] An indication that seems to substantiate this view is that the term *dhyāna* refers to a unique religious technique[39] used for spiritual cultivation, which was destined to be learned and practiced even by those belonging to the slave class. *Dhyāna* is a word translated into Chinese as "undisturbed cogitation."[40] It refers to how the condition of a scattered mind gets concentrated into a single point, and it can also refer to how this is learned and practiced.

Now, even with *dhyāna*, if one only trained in concentrating the scattered mind's condition into a single point, this would not be the equivalent of training to bring the self to completion.[41] If training consisted only of single-pointed concentration, then this would be a one-sided cultivation method. Why is it so? Because it would restrain the activity of the scattered mind. Since even the scattered mind is an activity of the mind, one also has to learn the activity of the scattered mind—that is, the activity of the distracted mind.[42] In other words, the condition of the mind concentrated in a single point needs to be reversed, in the opposite direction of an activity characterized by scattering. It is precisely by learning and practicing this way that the complete range of the activities of the mind can be understood. Because such a dynamic meaning was needed for true *dhyāna* and because the original (one-sided) *dhyāna* had to be called simply "*dhyāna*," the

About Tathāgata Zen

だから仏陀は在世中に弟子達に向かって、私の教える禅は単なる禅（即ち一方的な禅）ではなく如来如去の禅即ちタターガタの禅であると教え示したと如来禅では伝承して居る。タターガタと云う言葉は発音の仕方に依って、四つにも五つにも違った状態の意味を表す言葉とされて居る。如来と如去とは相対立する働きを意味して居ります。そう云う相対立する働きをタターガタが一人で現前して居ることを示しているのである。つまりタターアガタで一切の対立する働き、即ち生と滅、有と無、光明と暗黒と云う働きを云って居ることになります。すべてを内容として活動して居る者がタターアガタであります。そう云うわけでタターアガタ一切の勝者と意訳して居るのである。この一切の勝者を単に如来と云って居るのであります。如来如去の禅即ち如来禅とはどんな禅かこれで理解が出来たことになると存じます。

　釈迦牟尼は自ら弟子達に向かって自分は一切の勝者であるとか、あるいは如来であるとかと称したと伝承されて居るが、この如来と一切の勝者と云う意味の理解なしに禅を習ってはいけない。森の中に於いての六カ年の修行は悉達多のタターアガタの修行であったのである。タターアガタを知る智を得た悉達多は前に述べた通り、

special term of "thus coming and thus going *dhyāna*" (Tathāgata Zen) came to be formulated.

This is why Tathāgata Zen has handed down the idea that while Buddha was in this world he told his disciples, "The Zen that I teach is not simply Zen (namely, one-sided Zen). It is 'thus coming and thus going Zen,' in other words, Tathāgata Zen." Depending on how it is pronounced, the word Tathāgata expresses up to four or five meanings associated with different conditions. "Thus coming" and "thus going" denote two opposite activities. These opposite activities show that Tathāgata alone is manifesting. Namely, it refers to "Tathā-āgata,"[43] which means encompassing all opposing activities, such as life and annihilation, being and nonbeing, or light and darkness. Thus Tathā-āgata is the vibrant activity[44] that encompasses everything as its content. It is for this reason that the meaning of Tathā-āgata has been translated into Chinese as "the All Victorious One."[45] This All Victorious One is simply called "Tathāgata" (*nyorai*). I believe you have now understood what kind of Zen is meant by speaking of "thus coming and thus going Zen," or Tathāgata Zen.

It has been handed down that Śākyamuni turned to his disciples and called himself the All Victorious One and the Tathāgata. It is necessary to understand the meaning of these two expressions to study Zen. The six years of practice Siddhārtha spent in the woods were dedicated to the practice of Tathā-āgata. Once he had gained the wisdom allowing him to know Tathā-āgata, as mentioned above, Siddhārtha succeeded in expressing in words the activity of Tathāgata. Namely, the

About Tathāgata Zen   35

この森の中でタターガタの働きを言葉として歌うことに成功したのである。即ち一切の根元体はタターガタの光明と暗黒とが一体になって現れて居る究極（極現）の沈黙、即ちタターガタの体である。それは考える自己即ち我を消滅して現れた沈黙のタターガタであるから、これを「空」の働きをして居るタターガタの「体」の現前であるから空体の現前と云う。空体を誰も見る事は出来ない。空体を対象とする分別自己が現れると、この空体を色と見る。だからこの空体を色と命名するのである。

　物質とは何であるか、分別式が対象とする世界が物質界である。自己が物質界と関係を結ぶと空界が現れる。若し空界が現れなければその自己は未だ背後の世界を有って居る。だから空界が現れないのである。その背後の世界とも関係を結ぶと空界が現れる。それでこの空界の現前を沈黙のタターアガタの現前と云って居る。またこれを完全自己の現前と云って居る。分別自己即ち不完全自己が消滅して現れる自己が完全自己である。又完全智の現前である。

fundamental essence[46] of everything is the essence of the ultimate silence (ultimate manifestation) appearing when the light and darkness of the Tathāgata become one—in other words, it is the essence of the Tathāgata. This is the silent self who appears once the thinking self or the "I" (ga) has vanished. Because this is the silent Tathagatha that appears once the thinking self or the "I" (ga) has vanished and because this corresponds to the manifestation of the essence of the Tathāgata that produces the activity of emptiness, it is called the manifestation of the "empty essence" (kūtai).[47] No one can see the empty essence. When the discursive self[48] appears and considers the empty essence as an object, it sees the empty essence as "form." Hence, it is designated as "form."

What is "matter"? The world considered as object in discursive consciousness[49] constitutes the material world. The realm of emptiness[50] appears when the self establishes a relationship with the material world. If the realm of emptiness does not appear, it means that this self has not yet become part of the "world behind the scenes."[51] This is why the realm of emptiness does not appear. When establishing a relationship with that world behind the scenes, the realm of emptiness also appears. Thus, the manifestation of this realm of emptiness is also called the manifestation of Tathā-āgata. This is also called the manifestation of the complete self. The self that appears when the discursive self—also called incomplete self—vanishes is the complete self. It also is the manifestation of complete wisdom.

About Tathāgata Zen   37

ですから沈黙の如来の現前も完全自己の現前も何れも同じように無常の働きの賓と主とが一体を現前して居る当体であることを云って居るのである。賓主一体の体の外にはどんな物もないのである。それが全体である。しなければならぬと云う自己も、してはいけないと云う自己も、駄目であると云う自己も、よろしいと云う自己をもすべて解消して現れて居るのが完全自己の現前である。それは二つの対立する働き即ち生と死とが完全に一体を現前している状態で、完全に各々の性格を発揮する必要のない状態の現前である。ですからこれを意思意欲のない働きの現前と如来禅では云っておるのである。それが空の働きであり沈黙の現前である。即ち絶言絶慮の現前である。

　斯ういう賓主の対立する働きが空を現前して居る場合、賓主一体を現前するが飽くまでもそれは空体の現前である。これを理（理体）の現前と云って居るのが如来禅である。その空体を眺める者が消滅して居るのですから即ち自己は消滅して居るのであるから眺められる必要はない。然し賓主の分離に依って生まれた自己が賓と主とを眺めるのであるが、自己が賓と主とを完全に受容する働きをして現れて居る物が空と体の完全自己である。その完全自己は賓主一体の働きが現前する空の働きを内容として

For this reason it is said that the manifestation of the silent and still Tathāgata and the manifestation of the complete self are both in the same way the embodiment of the unity of the impermanent activity of guest and host. Nothing exists outside the embodiment of the unity of guest and host. That is, this is fundamental embodiment.[52] When the various selves saying "I have to," "I shouldn't," "It's hopeless," or "It's good," are totally eliminated, what appears is the manifestation of the complete self. This is a condition where the two opposite activities—namely life and death—have manifested their oneness: it constitutes the manifestation of a condition where there is absolutely no need for each one to display a distinctive character. In Tathāgata Zen this is described as the manifestation of the activity without will and desire. It constitutes the activity of emptiness and the manifestation of silence. In other words, this is the manifestation of release from language and discursive thinking.[53]

In the condition in which the opposing activities of guest and host are manifesting emptiness, the manifestation of the unification of guest and host is the ultimate manifestation of the empty essence.[54] Tathāgata Zen calls this the fundamental embodiment. Because the one contemplating this empty essence has vanished—namely because the self has vanished—there is no need to contemplate anything. Although the self resulting from the split between guest and host keeps contemplating both the guest and the host, what appears as the activity of the self completely adopting both guest and host is the complete self that is both empty and

About Tathāgata Zen

現れる事の現前である。ですから賓主一体が現前する生の働きを体とする空体の現前と同じ事を現前して居るのである。然し同じではあるが、存在者即ち自己の立場を主体として云う場合、この事を色と捉えて居るのが如来禅である。

　ですから極大の完全自己を極大の色体（物質）と呼んで居るのである。又極大の空体を空の理体と呼んで居るのである。逆に極大が収縮して極小の無常体即ち極小の空体を現前する。それを極小の空の理体と呼ぶ。又極小の空の色体とも呼んで居るのである。根元の状態は色でなく空でないかと考えられる疑念はこれで晴れたと思う。だから根元の色体は色体ではないのである。空体も然りで根元の空体は空体でもないのである。（ここを座禅をよくして下さい。）対象を絶している居る色体で即ち空体である。五蘊の色と一切を集め尽くして居る色と捉え色蘊と呼んで居るのである。ですから如来禅では結跏趺坐の座禅とはこの色体の現前であると教え示して居るのである。

rupa appears here 11 times see above.

embodied. This complete self is the manifestation of that which is appearing as the content of the activity of emptiness that is manifesting as the unification of guest and host. Therefore, it manifests the same thing as the manifestation of the empty essence, whose essence is the activity of life manifesting unification of guest and host. They are the same but Tathāgata Zen understands this as "form" when it speaks as the subject envisioning the standpoint of the existing entity—also called the self.

This is why the extremely large complete self is called the extremely large essence of form. Additionally, the extremely large empty essence is called the fundamental embodiment of emptiness. Conversely, when the extremely large contracts, it manifests the extremely small essence of impermanence—in other words, the extremely small empty essence.[55] This is called the fundamental essence of infinitesimal emptiness. It is also called the material essence of infinitesimal emptiness. I believe that this may have alleviated the doubts of those thinking that maybe the condition of the source (*kongen*) is not form but emptiness. Hence, concerning the source's material essence, it is *not* a material essence. The same thing can be said of the empty essence: concerning the source's empty essence, it is *not* an empty essence. (Please carefully consider this during zazen practice!) While being the material essence that cuts off particular objects, it is not different from the empty essence. It is called the aggregate of form based upon the understanding that it is the material form that exhaustively gathers the forms of the five aggregates. This is

About Tathāgata Zen 41

如来禅の呼吸禅はこの色体の爆発即ち結跏趺坐の爆発から始まるのである。ですから五蘊の教えを微細に研究したいと思うなら、修行者は如来禅の主唱する呼吸禅から這入らなかったらとても解るものではない。然し今はその暇がない。何故なら臨済の「四料揀」の提唱の要望があるからである。提唱と云うよりも講義と云うった方が可いと思う。そのためには如何しても五蘊の論理を微細に調べて自由自在に五蘊の教えを現前する能力を克ち得なかったら「四料揀」を玩具にしてしまうであろう。つまり子供の玩具と同じものになってしまうであろう。それを怖れるから、「四料揀」の講義の前に五蘊を説くのである。

　色とは一切を集め尽くして現れて居る一点を称して居るが、この色の声を聞く事のできない者は、色の体内に這入って色の声を聞けと如来禅者は云うのである。難しいことだ。然し禅者は何も難しい事はないと云う。色は自らの力で宇宙万物を形成して然る後に自らの力で極小の一点を現前して居るのである。だから難しいことはないのだと禅者は云って居るのである。自らの力とは何んな力ぞ、生と滅の力である。即ち色は生と滅の力を内容として色の

why in Tathāgata Zen it is taught that zazen in the full lotus position is the manifestation of this material essence.

The breathing Zen technique of Tathāgata Zen begins with the explosion of this material essence, namely with the explosion of the full lotus position. Thus, if practitioners want to meticulously investigate the teaching of the five aggregates, unless they start with the breathing Zen technique advocated in Tathāgata Zen it is unlikely they will gain any understanding. Now, there is no time for this, however. This is because there was a request for Dharma instructions (*teishō*) on Linji's Four Conditions.[56] Rather than speaking of Dharma instructions I think that it would be better to mention lectures. For this purpose, one way or another, without meticulously examining the logic of the five aggregates and without gaining the ability to freely manifest the teaching of the five aggregates, it will likely lead to reducing these Four Conditions to mere toys, nothing more than children's toys. It is because I am afraid of this that before giving a lecture on the Four Conditions I will explain the five aggregates.

Regarding the meaning of "form," followers of Tathāgata Zen say, "For those who cannot hear the sound of this form called the one point appearing where everything has been exhaustively gathered, enter within a body of form and listen!" It is something difficult. Yet Zen practitioners claim that nothing is difficult. Through its own power, form gives shape to all things in the universe, and then through its own power manifests one infinitesimal point. This is why Zen practitioners claim that nothing is difficult. What on earth

About Tathāgata Zen 43

体内に宿って居るのである。云うならば膨張と収縮の力である。即ち如来と如去の働きである。怖ろしいことだ。色と云う自己は自己を二分する。膨張と収縮と云う（生と死と云う）相対立する働きを内容として居るのである。然し怖れることはない。生と死との力は性格は違うが力即ち力量は平等で色と云う自己の体内で安らかに休息して居るからである。

　然しながら滅即ち死の働きの究極の住居場所は、極小の宇宙であるから、何時もそうした極小の宇宙を現前しようとして居る。これに対して膨張即ち生の働きは極大という究極の状態を現前しようとして居る。それが生の住居場所である。斯うした二つの対立をする厄介な生と滅の働きを色と云う自己は内容として居るから、おそろしいことだと云うのである。

　人間も動物もすべて存在して居るものは欲望を有って居ると云っても可い。欲望があるから成長発達するのであると云ってよいのである。ところがその欲望を起こすなと否定するものがある。それが反対の心の働きと云うことになるのである。だから生と死との働きは自己否定と自己肯定をする自己の心の働きと見てもよかろう。何れにしよ色と云う自己は色を形成する働きを内容として居る。

is this power called "own power"? It is the power of life and annihilation. In other words, form has the power of life and annihilation as its content, and dwells within a body of form. This could be described as the power of expansion and contraction. In other words, the activity of thus coming and thus going. That's frightening! The self known as "form" is dividing itself into two pieces. Its content is made of the opposite activities of expansion and contraction or life and death. But one should not be afraid. The reason is that the power of life and the power of death have distinctive characters, but in regard to their respective power—in other words their potency—both are equal and they peacefully rest within the body of the self called "form."

Nonetheless, since the ultimate place where the activity of annihilation—namely death—resides is the infinitesimal universe, this activity tends to constantly manifest the infinitesimal universe. Conversely, expansion—namely the activity of life—tends to manifest the ultimate condition of the extremely large. This is the place where life resides. Because the self identified as "form" is made of these two opposing and troublesome activities of annihilation and life, it is sometimes called "frightening."

We can consider that human beings and animals, all existing entities have desires. It is possible to say that they grow up and develop because these desires exist. Even so, some entity may deny it and say, "Don't produce desire!" This indicates the opposite activity of the mind. Thus, the activities of life and death can be viewed as the activities of the self's mind,

About Tathāgata Zen   45

そうして働きは相対立する二つの働きであることと云うまでもない。それがタターガタとタターアガタと唱えたのが悉達多であると如来禅では伝承して居るのである。
　然るにタターガタは如来と如去の二つの働きをする。そのようにこの色は二つの働きをする、心と云うかタターガタと云うかそう云う働きを内容として色を形成して居るのである。たとえば色と云う自己が自己否定の働きをして極小と云う立場を現前して住居場所を現前する場合がある。いうまでもなくそれは収縮の働きが積極的に活動して色の住居場所を現前することで、極小の宇宙がすべての現前である。この場合、自己肯定膨張の働きを喜んで否定の働き即ち死の働きに随順して極小の居住場所を現前する。そこで主、即ち死する働きは死する働きを休止する。死する働きに随順した賓の働き即ち生の働きも休止する。
　然し極小の住居場所は膨張の働き即ち生の働きの本来の住居場所ではない。直ちに目を醒して本来の住居場所を建設するべく活動を開始する。そうすると主、即ち収縮も目を醒して行動を開始する。ここで対立の場が現れる。遂に賓と主とは対立分離する。これを色自体を二分する

denying itself or approving itself. In any case, the self called "form" has the activity of giving shape to form as its content. Obviously, such activity consists of two opposite activities. In Tathāgata Zen it has been handed down that Siddhārtha formulated the expressions "Tathāgata" and "Tathā-āgata" to describe them.

In spite of that, the Tathāgata performs the two activities of "thus coming" and "thus going." In a similar way, this "form" performs two activities: whether we want to call it "the mind" or "the Tathāgata," it has this activity as its content and gives shape to form. For instance, there is the case when the self called "form" performs the activity of denying itself, thus manifesting the standpoint of the infinitesimal and manifesting its dwelling. Obviously, this corresponds to the activity of contraction becoming positively active, which manifests the entirety of the infinitesimal universe by manifesting the dwelling of "form." In this case, it manifests the dwelling of the infinitesimal by rejoicing at the activity of the self-approving expansion, while being subordinate to the activity of denial—corresponding to death. There, the host—namely the activity of death—suspends the activity of death. The activity of the guest who was subordinate to the activity of death—namely the activity of life—is also suspended.

Yet the dwelling of the infinitesimal is not the original dwelling of the activity of expansion—namely the activity of life. It immediately wakes up, and starts becoming active with the aim of constructing its original dwelling. Then the host—namely contraction—wakes up as well and becomes active.

About Tathāgata Zen   47

働き即ち賓主分離の現前云って居る。主と賓とか分離すると云うことは賓と主との間に空間を造ることである。賓と主との間に空間が生まれなかったら賓と主とは分離することはない。然らばその空間は何処から来たのかと云うことになる。云う迄もなく賓主とが共に有っていた大空間を、共に放出して空間を造作するのである。その場合賓と主との間に露われた空間は自火の性を醸し出す現れる。つまり五十人と五十人とが対立して綱引きをすると綱は最中から煙を出して火を造り出して綱を切断する。その様に賓の有の空間と主の有の空間が分離する場合。空間は火の玉となって現れる。この空間と体として存在者は自己を形成するのである。

　賓主分離の働きに依って生まれた空間を体として、存在者は自己を形成することになるが存在者（自己）が生まれた場合、その自己は賓と主とから関係を断絶して生まれるのである。賓や主と若し生まれる存在者が（子）が関係を続ける場合、それは未だ生まれて居ないのである。例えば賓が余りにも強いために生まれる子が賓と関係を結ぶなら生まれることは出来ない。それは内なる主との関係も然りである。賓主分離の働きに依って生まれる存在者は必ず賓と主とが断絶して生まれるのである。だから生まれ

At this point a locus of opposition appears. Eventually, the guest and the host oppose each other and split. This is called the activity of form dividing itself into two—namely the manifestation of guest and host splitting. To say that the guest and the host split implies the creation of an empty space between the host and the guest. If it was not for the emergence of an empty space between the guest and the host, there would be no split between them. Well, this is the proper place to ask where the empty space came from. Needless to say that guest and host created this space by abandoning together the greater space in which they existed.[57] In this case the empty space that surfaced between guest and host also produced their individual natures. In other words, it evokes a scene where fifty people are opposing fifty other people playing a tug of war, when smoke comes from the middle of the rope and it creates flames that sever the rope. Similarly, when the empty space of "being" that belongs to the guest and the empty space of "being" that belongs to the host are divided, this empty space appears as a fireball. The existing entity uses this empty space as its essence, thus giving shape to its self.[58]

The existing entity gives shape to its self by using as its "essence" the empty space generated thanks to the separation between guest and host; but in regard to the situation when the existing entity (the self) is born, this self emerges by breaking off its relation with both guest and host. If this born existing entity (child) continued its relation with either the guest or the host, it would mean that it was still unborn. For instance, if because the guest was too powerful the child

About Tathāgata Zen 49

た子は賓にも主にも属さないと云う立場に立って生まれることになるのである。

　自己は光輝く存在者として生まれる。しかしその光明は無論自己の体となって現れる。空体即ち如去と如来とが一体となって現れる賓主一体の「体」即ち「空」であるが、その空の当体が二つに分離した場合に現れる光明であると伝承して居るのが如来禅である。だから生まれた自己は賓と主と関係を結んで光明を消さないようにしなければならない。つまり光明とは生まれた自己が必要とする食物であると如来禅では捉えて居るのである。

　賓と主との分離に依って生まれた自己は必ず積極的に活動する賓の性格を受けて賓に随順する。そこで賓の有って居る空間を克ち取って光明を発する。その場合自己は主の立場を退けて居ることになる。若し主に随順すれば賓主分離の完成はないことになる。このように、自己が生まれて、賓と主との断絶の関係を有すると自己は主を

to be were to establish a relation with the guest, it could not be born. The same thing can be said about the relation with the host inside. The existing entity born thanks to the separation between guest and host necessarily has to be born after breaking off with guest and host. Thus, it means that when the child is born it does so from a standpoint where it has no affiliation, neither with the guest nor with the host.

The self is born as a luminous entity. This light appears as the essence of the self. Tathāgata Zen has handed down the idea that the "empty essence"—the essence resulting from the oneness[59] between guest and host when the "thus gone" and the "thus come" become one—namely, what corresponds to emptiness—is the light appearing when the emptiness of this very essence separates into two. This is why the arisen self must avoid extinguishing the light, by establishing a relation with the guest and the host. Tathāgata Zen understands such "light" as the food needed by the arisen self.

The self, which arose thanks to the separation between the guest and the host, necessarily receives the distinctive character of the guest who is positively active, and is subordinate to the guest. This is where the self procures the empty space belonging to the guest and produces light. In this case the self is avoiding the standpoint of the host. If it were to be subordinate to the host, the completion of the separation between guest and host could not occur. Thus, the self is born and once it has acquired a relation characterized by breaking off with guest and host, the self avoids the host and becomes subordinate to the guest. Even when speaking of the

About Tathāgata Zen 51

退けて賓に随順する。自己が賓に随順すると云っても、自己は未だ認識作用は勿論感覚作用すら完全でない。

　賓主分離の働きに依って自己が生まれた場合情熱と云って可い独特の感情と自己を成立させる空間は受容して生まれると云ったが、そうした情熱の働き者として生まれるだけでありとても認識作用の能力など勿論ないのである。五蘊ではこの情熱の働きを「受」と云って居る。今日の仏教学者の中には哲学の影響を受けて、この受を印象作用と云う風に解して居る学者も居る。扱て何う云うものであろうか？

　賓主分離の働きには必ず限界が起こる。賓と主との対立は賓が賓の究極を現前するまで活動しようとする積極性を以て主と対立する働きである。対立の影響を受けて、賓と主とは一気に極大と極小の分離を現前することはない。必ず分離の働きの限界を現前して一時仮の休息を現前する。休息から醒めると新しい賓主の対立が起きる。つまり賓主分離の働きを続けることによって賓主一体と云う働きを起す。これは全く矛盾した働きと云わねばなるまい。

self becoming subordinate to the guest, of course, the self still has not fully acquired a cognitive function, and not even a sensory function.

In the case where the self was born thanks to the activity of separation between guest and host, I say that it is born after having adopted a distinctive emotion that can be characterized as fervor and also after having adopted the empty space formative of the self. But this only means that it was born as an activity full of such fervor, and it obviously does not have the least capability for cognitive function. In the language of the five aggregates, the activity of this fervor is called sensation.[60] Some contemporary Buddhist scholars have been influenced by philosophy, interpreting sensation as "the operation of impressions." Well, what does it refer to, then?

In the activity of the separation between guest and host, without fail a limit arises. The opposition between guest and host is characterized by aggressiveness, which pushes the guest toward remaining active until it has manifested the guest's apex and whose activity opposes the host's. Having received the influence of their mutual opposition, the guest and the host never manifest the separation between the extremely large and the extremely small. Without fail when the activity of separation reaches a limit, a temporary moment of rest is manifested. Waking up from this moment of rest, a new opposition between guest and host arises. In other words an activity arises in which guest and host are unified in that they continue the activity of the separation between guest and host. One has to recognize that these are completely paradoxical activities.

About Tathāgata Zen   53

何故なら分離の働きを至当とすれば、一体を現前する働きは不当と云って可い働きを現前するからである。つまり主の収縮の働きが膨張しなければ賓主一体と云うことは起こり得ないからである。膨張の働きは膨張の究極を現前しようとして居るのであるから、極小の根元に無論戻る事はない。若し膨張が逆戻りするなら、これ又矛盾する働きをすることになり理に適わぬ働きとなる。この矛盾の働きを如何理解すべきか、修行者が泣かねばならぬ立場に立つとせば、斯うした立場に立つからであろう。然るに斯うした矛盾を矛盾とせず、当然の理として矛盾を突破して賓主は一体を現前する。そして根元の賓主一体即ち色の立場を一位とするならば二位の根元の立場即ち唯一界を現前するのである。斯うした賓主分離と賓主一体の繰り返しを無量無数重ねて膨張の働きは究極を現前する。それが五蘊と云って居る識である。 VIJNANA

斯うして賓主分離と賓主一体の繰り返しを重ねて行く間に愛の働きは想の働きに発達する。つまり賓主分離を新しく展開する度び毎に新しく生まれる自己は主を退けて賓に随順しなければならぬと云う経験をする。そうした経験を修行者は何千回と経験するであろう。主を退けて

It is because if one views the activity of separation as reasonable, then the activity of manifesting oneness is an activity that can be considered unreasonable.[61] In other words, if the host's activity of contraction does not expand, the oneness between guest and host cannot happen. Since the activity of expansion tends to manifest as the apex of expansion, obviously, it will not return to the source (*kongen*) of the infinitesimal. If expansion were to turn back, this would also constitute a paradoxical activity, an activity that does not conform to reason. How should we understand such paradoxical activities? If one adopts the position of a practitioner who must be crying, then the problem results precisely from having adopted such a position. On the other hand, if one does not consider the paradox as a paradox but rather as an obvious principle, then one breaks through the paradox and one manifests the unity of guest and host. In this way, through countless and incalculable replications of these processes of the guest and host being separated and then becoming one again, the activity of expansion manifests its apex. This constitutes the aggregate of consciousness, listed among the five aggregates.

While repeating the separation between guest and host, the activity of attachment[62] develops into the activity known as perception.[63] In other words, each time a new separation between guest and host unfolds, the self who is born anew creates the experience of avoiding the host and being subordinate to the guest. Practitioners will have had such an experience thousands of times. It creates a strong cognitive function based on the awareness that one has to avoid the host and be

About Tathāgata Zen 55

賓に随順しなければならぬと云う強い認識作用が生まれてくる。これが前に述べたアートマン即ち我である。斯うした我の発見を以て禅としてはいけないことは云うまでもなかろう。斯うした我の立場の主張が強ければ強い程、賓主一体の場に臨んだ場合、必ず苦悶に出会っていないのでないか。

　何故に自己は抹殺されねばならないのか。自己は賓主分離の世界の修行に於いて完全に賓の立場を克ち取る修行をして居る。然るに何故にそうした自己を抹殺せねばならぬのか。これに対する答えは余りにも簡単と云ってよい。退けるものがある限り自己は退ける者のために抹殺されるのである。自己が退けねばならぬ者は、自己と対立するものである。自己を護ってくれる世界を有つことは自己に取って力強いことである。そう云う自己の世界や団体に立って、対立者を退けることは面白いことであるかもしれない。然し対立者が無くなるわけではないのである。対立者が居る間は安心することは出来ない。退けてきた対立者をよくよく考えてみれば自己と同居していた友であり母なのである。そのことに気が付いたなら自己は喜んで進んで抹殺の道に進むであろう。即ち自ら進んで退いた者の内容者になろうと云う道を歩むように自己の

subordinate to the guest. This is what was described above as the *ātman* or the "I." Needless to say, from the Zen perspective this discovery of the "I" should not be made. Isn't it clear that the stronger the affirmation of this ego's standpoint, the more inevitable it becomes that it will encounter agony when facing the locus of oneness between guest and host?[64]

Why is it that the self must be wiped out? Through its practice in the world of separation between guest and host, the self performs a type of practice enabling it to completely procure the standpoint of the guest. Why should such a self be wiped out, then? One could say that the answer to this question is extremely simple. As long as it has something to avoid, the self is being wiped out because of the one it was trying to avoid. What the self has to avoid is what opposes the self. For the self, having a world that protects it is reassuring. From the perspective of such a world of the self or from the perspective of a group, avoiding opponents may appear preferable. Yet opponents will not disappear. And as long as there are opponents, one cannot find inner peace. Upon careful reflection, the opponents that one was trying to avoid were living together with the self: they were friends, they were one's mother. Once it has become aware of this, the self will happily proceed onto the path where it will be wiped out. Namely, it will reverse[65] the path trodden by the self by spontaneously proceeding to walk the path where it becomes the content of the person it has tried to avoid.

This has been exposed by Śākyamuni, who explained it as engaging on the path of selflessness. This is nothing but

About Tathāgata Zen   57

歩む道を転ずるであろう。

　これを釈迦牟尼は無我道の実践として歌ったのである。つまりアートマンの抹殺である。ここに至って仏教のアートマンの捉え方と自己の捉え方とが判っきりしてくるであろう。アートマンは賓主分離の世界に於いて必ず肯定して育て上げねばならぬ問題である。然しアートマンの肯定を以て至上としたならば、対立の働きと永遠に対立することになる。アートマンを肯定することに依って、退けて居る考えを、それを見る目が開かなかったら、それはアートマンの考えに捉われて居ることになる。即ち無常を観ずる人にはなれまい。

　扨て賓主分離と賓主一体の繰り返しを重ねることによって自己は無我道を実践しなければならんと云う強い意志を以つということになる。強い意思を以って無我道を実践するその行為を五蘊では行と歌って居るのである。その強い意志を菩提心とも云って居る。

wiping out the ātman. At this stage, the understanding of the ātman in the Buddha teachings and the understanding of the self are probably becoming clear. The issue of the ātman needs to be raised[66] in an affirmative way within the context of the world of separation between guest and host. If the affirmation of the ātman were to become supreme, it would forever stand apart from the activity of opposition. But if by affirming the ātman the seeing eye[67] does not open to the thoughts it was trying to avoid, it means that one has become captive to the idea of the ātman. In that case, one cannot become cognizant of impermanence.

Through added repetitions of division and unification of guest and host, the self has acquired the strong determination that it must engage on the path of selflessness. The action of engaging on the path of selflessness with a strong determination corresponds to the "volitional formations"[68] explained in the five aggregates. This strong determination is called *bodhicitta*, or awakening resolve.

This is a translation of *Nyoraizen ni tsuite* 如来禅に就いて by Sasaki Jōshū Rōshi 佐々木承周老師, received on May 25, 2013, from Myōren Yasukawa, the Rōshi's Inji, at Rinzai-ji Zen Center in Los Angeles.

About Tathāgata Zen

Notes

1. Although *bukkyō* 仏教 is usually translated as "Buddhism" or "Buddhist teachings," this passage emphasizes the literal meaning of "teachings [given by] an awakened being" and downplays any association with a particular religion.
2. *Jōtai* 状態 is one of the key words used throughout this text. It is translated as "state," "condition," "situation," or "circumstances."
3. In this opening section Jōshū Rōshi is using the contrast between sleeping and waking on three levels: 1) the common understanding, 2) as a metaphor for the states of ignorance and enlightenment, and 3) as a metaphor for the complete unification of nonduality in contrast to dualistic consciousness. *[i.e., oneness]*
4. The key Buddhist expression *genzen suru* 現前する is translated as "to manifest." (The noun *genzen* means "manifestation" or "actualization.") The closely related verb *arawareru* 現れる has been translated as "to appear."
5. The Japanese expression for "dreaming" literally means "seeing dreams" (*yume miru* 夢見る). To make the explanation intelligible in English, the literal construction of the sentence has been retained.
6. The Japanese verb for "coming back to life" (*yomigaeru* 蘇る) literally means "to be reborn." This language should not be confused with Christian terminology.
7. The translation "learning and practice" has been used for the Japanese compound 修習, read *shujū* as a Buddhist term and *shūshū* as a common noun. Here, it seems to have been used as a common noun. When used as a Buddhist term, translations include "cultivation," "training," and "study." Those who engage in practice are simply "practitioners" (*shujūsha* 修習者). When used as a verb (*shujū suru* 修習する), it has been translated as "to cultivate."

8. The verb translated as "to posit" (*hyōsen* 表詮) is a term used in Buddhist logic, where it refers to making a statement.
9. In Buddhist and pre-Buddhist Chinese texts the term translated as "activity" or "activities" (*hataraki* 働き) is often written with the Chinese character 用, also read *hataraki*. In Japanese, this evokes "work" or "labor" because the verb *hataraku* means "to work." Alternative translations would be "way(s) of functioning" or "working(s)." Jōshū Rōshi's text alludes to the "essence-function" or "embodiment-manifestation" (*taiyū* 體用) paradigm, which dates back to the third-century Profound Learning (*xuanxue* 玄學) movement in China, or Neo-Daoism.
10. The Japanese expression *mujun shita* 矛盾した can be understood as either "contradictory" or "paradoxical," but the latter makes more sense in this context.
11. The translation "very essence" (*tōtai* 当体) attempts to convey how the essential nature becomes present and tangible.
12. Although *jibun* 自分 can refer simply to "oneself," it is used here in an impersonal way to indicate one's true nature.
13. The translation "functioning of consciousness" corresponds to the Japanese *ishiki sayō* 意識作用, which is also often rendered as the "operation of consciousness," in the sense of the functioning of the mind. The compound *sayō* is closely related to the key word "activity" (*hataraki*) used throughout this text.
14. The idea here is that when a self is *trying* to do what the Tathāgata activity is spontaneously doing, then it becomes difficult to relate to others in a genuine fashion. Personal will and desire are overlaid onto an activity that has none, and this causes all kinds of preferences.
15. This distinction between "incomplete" (*fukanzen* 不完全) and "complete" (*kanzen* 完全) could also be translated as "imperfect" and "perfect."
16. The Chinese character 智 (*chi*), which we translate here as "cognitive acuity," is often used in Sino-Japanese sources to convey *prajñā*.
17. Complete wisdom (*kanzen chi* 完全知) refers to perceiving things as they are and not to "knowledge."
18. Jōshū Rōshi coined this expression, translated here as "ceaselessly refining ourselves" (*todomaru koto naku kōshū suru* 留まることなく更修する). The first clause literally means "without stopping"; the second section can be understood in various ways. The verb *kōshū suru* 更修する means "to refine" in the sense of seeking improvement by correcting oneself.
19. Jōshū Rōshi makes a unique distinction between the two aspects translated here as "reality" (*jitsu* 実) and "guest" (*hin* 賓). The more common distinction is that between guest and "host" or "master" (*shu* 主). Jōshū Rōshi's substitution of "reality" where one would expect to find "host" implies that he considers the host to be the underlying reality of our experience.
20. The Chinese compound translated as "obliteration" (*inmetsu* 隠滅) includes the nuances of hiding as well as annihilation and disappearance. The second character is also translated as "cessation," especially when it corresponds to the Sanskrit *nirodha*.
21. This implicit recognition is expressed by the clause *an'anri ni shōchi shite ita* 暗々裡に承知していた, which could also be translated as "he was tacitly aware."

[Handwritten note at top: My copy of The Recorded Sayings of .... Lin Chi is published by the Institute for Zen Studies, Hanazono College (no mention of Kirchner).]

22. The terms "guest and host" first appear in the ninth-century Zen classic, *Rinzai roku*, published in English as *The Record of Linji*, translated by Ruth Fuller Sasaki and edited by Thomas Yūhō Kirchner (Honolulu: University of Hawaii Press, 2009), 133–34. Often understood to mean "objective and subjective," these terms can also imply the contrast between incomplete and complete manifestation, as they do in section IV, 132–33.

23. The "standpoint of the source" (*kongen no tachiba* 根源の立場) is a phrase that Jōshū Rōshi often uses to communicate the experience of being grounded completely in the activity of impermanence, the underlying activity of the cosmos and of consciousness. *[marginal note: important]*

24. The verb translated here as "to produce" (*zōsa suru* 造作) refers to the creative process. The word "annihilation" (*metsu* 滅) can also refer to "cessation," for example in the Four Noble Truths, or may simply indicate death.

25. Interestingly, the Chinese compound translated as "one-sided" (*katawa* 片輪) literally means "crippled" and indicates defective "wheels," with only one side functioning.

26. The phrase the "original self" (*honrai no jiko* 本来の自己) recalls the famous phrase from Case 23 of the classic koan collection, the *Mumonkan*, in which the newly minted Sixth Patriarch Eno (Huineng) suddenly asks a monk who has been chasing him, "What is your original face (*honrai no mimoku* 本来の目目)?" It is one of many allusions to the constantly changing activity of impermanence. Jōshū Rōshi's phrase emphasizes how this is not an abstract concept but is grounded in our moment-to-moment experience.

27. The verb translated as "to attain" (*kachieru* 克ち得る) carries the nuance of something that has been obtained at great cost, as in a victory won against an opponent or overcoming adversity.

28. The Japanese expression (*shamon* 沙門) corresponds to the Sanskrit *śramaṇa*, originally indicating religious practitioners who renounced their worldly life to strive for liberation and usually lived as mendicants.

29. The standard translation for the five *skandhas* (*goun* 五蘊) is "five aggregates"; the five categories describe how the fabricated self is constructed.

30. The word translated as "traditions" (*kyōha* 教派) literally indicates "teaching factions or branches." If may refer to different Buddhist schools or to different schools of thought within a single tradition such as Zen.

31. The word translated as "secret" (*hiketsu* 秘訣) usually refers to a "secret formula" or key to understanding something, while the expression rendered as "imparted from teacher to disciple" (*denju* 伝授) indicates a process of direct initiation and transmission.

32. Here, the Sanskrit *rūpa* (*shiki* 色) is translated as "form"; it is often translated as "material form."

33. The Japanese verb used here (*tabaneru* 束ねる) is written in the katakana syllabary for emphasis. It means to bundle something up, or to tie something up in a bundle.

34. Translated as "chaotic" here, the word *midareru* 乱れる implies confusion and disorder. In this context it refers to how the mind scatters in many directions, as indicated by the verb *sanran shite* 散乱して, which means "to scatter."

Notes   63

35. Jōshū Rōshi provides parenthetical glosses to explain the implications of his use of the verb usually translated as "to hold" (*hajū suru* 把住する), which in modern Japanese implies "to seize." He suggests "to hold" (*tsukamu* つかむ) and "to envelop" (*hōyō* 包容), hence the translation "embrace."
36. Here the expression "learning to practice" (*shūshū* 修習) refers to learning the practice of zazen, which unifies a scattered mind.
37. Usually the expression translated as "practical learning" (*jisshū* 実習) simply refers to the practical application of what has been learned through teachings. It is sometimes simply translated as "practice," but we need to differentiate this from "practice" (*shugyō* 修行), understood as cultivation. A similar expression, *jitsugaku* 実学, is also often translated as "practical learning."
38. This passage seems to be based on the Indo-Aryan migration hypothesis, popular in the early twentieth century, which posited that a wave of immigration from Indo-Aryans contributed to the demise of the earlier Indus civilization and coincided with the emergence of Vedic culture. It is now more common to speak of Proto-Indo-Iranians but the term Aryans has been kept in the translation to reflect the terminology used in the original Japanese text.
39. The translation "religious technique" (*shūhō* 宗法) is an approximation for a method based on a certain principle, regardless of the misleading nuances conveyed by the English word "religious." The expression translated as "cultivation" (*shūyō* 修養) conveys a nuance that is slightly different from the other expressions encountered so far, in the sense that it includes both the idea of practice and of "raising" or "nourishing" someone.
40. The expression "undisturbed cogitation" is a translation for the Chinese compound pronounced *jōryo* 静慮 in Japanese, which could also be translated literally as "quiet thinking."
41. To "bring to completion" (*kanzen ni shiageru* 完全に仕上げる) refers to realization. The word translated as "training" (*shūren* 修練) is another instance of "practice," in this instance based on the metaphor of a blacksmith melting and hammering a piece of iron.
42. This "activity of the distracted mind" (*kokoro no sanman suru hataraki* 心の散漫する働き) suggests random thoughts and a mental condition characterized by its lack of focus.
43. The spelling of "Tathā-āgata" follows the entry in *Kōsetsu bukkyōgo daijiten* 広説佛教語大辞典, edited by Nakamura Hajime 中村元 (Tokyo: Tōkyō shoseki, 2001), 1,146, entry 多他阿伽陀. Jōshū Rōshi wrote it in katakana (タターアガタ), which would correspond to "Tathā-agata."
44. The phrase *katsudō* 活動 (literally "living movement") is often translated as "activity." In order to differentiate it from the translation "activity" or "activities" corresponding to *hataraki* in this text, we have translated it as "vibrant activity."
45. The translation "all victorious" (*issai no shōsha* 一切の勝者) reflects one nuance of this expression where the accent is put on the idea of the "victor," whereas the second part of the Chinese translation often simply refers to "the most excellent."
46. The idea of a "fundamental essence" (*kongentai* 根元体) is unusual in Buddhist terminology. It should be noted that the expression "become one" (*ittai* 一体) also

includes the same Chinese character for body that has been translated as "essence." In Chinese this literally means to form one body with something, or to embody it.

47. The translation "empty essence" (*kūtai* 空体) preserves the symmetry with "material essence" (*shikitai* 色体). When speaking of "emptiness," keep in mind Nāgārjuna's precise definition of *śūnyatā* as the "absence of intrinsic or independent existence" (*svabhāva*); in other words, it is an expression of the fundamental interrelatedness of all things and experiences.

48. The "discursive self" (*funbetsu jiko* 分別自己) indicates the dualistic self that analyzes and discriminates between opposites.

49. Here *funbetsu shiki* 分別式 (discursive mode) is translated as 分別識 (discursive consciousness); that is, the dualistic consciousness in the world of self and other.

50. In this context emphasis is placed on the contrast between physical reality (the material world) and emptiness, so the expression "realm of emptiness" has been chosen to translate *kūkai* 空界. It should be noted, however, that in Chinese Buddhist literature this expression often merely indicates "the realm of space" or "open space."

51. This is an unusual phrase in Jōshū Rōshi's teaching. Three notes to keep in mind: 1) The "realm of emptiness" is not a physical space: it is a mode of cognition in which the empty activity of the self and Tathāgata are experienced together; 2) If it does not appear, this is the common experience we normally have of the world: it is the exclusively dualistic material world; 3) If this realm has not yet appeared, the self has not yet (*mada* 未だ) experienced the "world behind the scenes" of the material world—that is, the "host" behind the "guest."

52. *Ritai* 理體 is a challenging term to translate. "Principle" or "pattern" (*ri*) is dynamic, not static; *tai*, which philosophically means "essence," phenomenologically means "to embody." Jōshū Rōshi uses this term to describe deep experience: *ritai* indicates an embodied or experienced dynamic principle, thus it is translated as "fundamental embodiment."

53. The translation "release from language and discursive thinking" (*zetsugon zetsuryo* 絶言絶慮) literally means "cutting off words, cutting off discursive thinking." In classic Buddhist literature the same idea is also conveyed by the four characters meaning "freed from language and discursive thinking" (*rigon zetsuryo* 離言絶慮).

54. "Empty essence" (*kutai* 空體) also carries the connotation of "the embodiment of emptiness."

55. The "extremely large"(*gyokudai* 極大) and the "extremely small"(*gyokusho* 極小) are the zenith of expansion and the nadir of contraction, respectively. They are constantly alternating to generate our spheres of experience.

56. The Four Conditions (*shiryōken* 四料揀) taught by Rinzai Zen have also been translated as Four Classifications or Four Alternatives. See *The Record of Linji*, 150–53. An interpretive paraphrasing is: 1) Taking away the person (the subjective world) but not the surroundings (the objective world); 2) Taking away the objective but not the subjective; 3) Taking away both subjective and objective; 4) Taking away neither subjective nor objective.

57. The verb "to abandon" (*hōridasu* 放り出す) implies giving up or throwing out something.

Notes 65

58. It is through this process that the momentary self we experience all the time arises. Through this struggle between the activities of expansion and contraction—guest and host—the discursive self arises and manifests our daily worlds or spheres of experience.
59. The expression translated throughout this text as "oneness" or "to become one" (*ittai* 一体) literally means "one body" or "one essence." Hence, the passage rendered as "the essence resulting from the oneness" literally corresponds to "the 'body' in [the expression] 'one body.'"
60. "Sensation" is a standard translation for the Sanskrit *vedanā-skandha*, sometimes translated as "feeling." It was translated into Chinese as *shou* 受 (Japanese *ju*), which conveys the nuance of "reception" and indicates the "taste" of each experience: pleasant, unpleasant, or neutral.
61. That is, if one thinks the activity of separation is reasonable, that it can occur, one also tends to think that it is not reasonable or possible for separation and unification to both be able to happen within the same sphere of our experience.
62. The word translated as "attachment" (*ai* 愛) is a Buddhist term with negative connotations. It should not be confused with the modern Japanese meaning of "love." In some cases, as above, it can also be translated as "affection."
63. The aggregate translated as "perception" (*sō* 想) corresponds to the Sanskrit *samjñā*, which is often translated as "ideation," referring to thoughts that surface together. The word *samjñā* includes the nuance of "mutual agreement" and "sharing the same opinion," which translates into associative thoughts.
64. This is a complicated passage that could be interpreted as follows: The host or master is the ground of our experience, with which we are one at all times. It is experience without self-objectification. It is what could be called "no-person" experience: spontaneous experience without self-identification or attachment. The "guest" is what takes this no-person experience as its object. The personal self arises when the guest and host become separate and the guest takes the host as its object. This forms the ego or the "I" or the *ātman*—all three terms mean the same thing. The ego is in agony when facing the locus of the oneness of guest and host because it is realizing its own apparent separation from this experience of unity.
65. The verb "to reverse" or "to transform" (*tenzuru* 転ずる) conveys the literal sense of the revolution of a wheel. Here it implies a complete reversal of the normal activity of the incomplete self. It calls to mind a phrase from the *Lankavatara Sutra*: *āśraya-parāvrtti*, "a turning around of the base of consciousness," the result of intense meditation practice, which destroys the impurities (*kleśas*) and recognizes the emptiness of all things and experiences. See Charles Prebish, *Buddhism: A Modern Perspective* (University Park: Pennsylvania State University Press, 1975), 115–16.
66. Here the verb "to raise" (*sodate ageru* 育て上げる) is used in the sense of "raising" or "nursing" a child.
67. The "seeing eye" (*miru me* 見る目) suggests an awakened perspective.
68. The translation "volitional formations" or "formations" (*gyō* 行) corresponds to the Sanskrit *samskāra*. It is also translated as "constructional activities" and includes states that initiate action, such as volition (*cetanā*).

66

Afterword

In June we held a workshop on the *Diamond Sutra* at the Rinzai-ji Zen Center in Los Angeles. Roshi was feeling weak at the beginning of the weekend: after all, he turned 107 in April. Although he was not taking part in the workshop, we hoped that he might get the "vibe" from the thirty-five active participants. Sure enough, vibe or not, by the end of the weekend Roshi was giving a group *sanzen* (semi-private koan interviews) to a few monks and students who had stayed at the Zen Center after the workshop. Two days later he decided to take a road trip to Phoenix to be present when his disciple Sōkai Geoffrey Barrett ordained his successor at the Haku-un-ji Zen Center. Roshi had not left California in two and a half years due to failing health, which had also prevented him from teaching.

Why would a 107-year-old Zen master take an eight-hour road trip? This sounds like a koan, but it's actually a simple question with a straightforward answer. Roshi is completely devoted to teaching and to his students. That's why this is the first authorized publication to come from Roshi's hand. While from time to time his Dharma talks (*teishō*) have been published, in his fifty-two years of teaching in the West he has never before published a book. (An unauthorized volume of Dharma talks from a 1973 Lama Foundation *sesshin* was published as *Buddha Is the Center of Gravity*, but the translations are uneven.) His complete attention has been focused on the more than eight hundred *sesshins*, five thousand Dharma talks, and two hundred and fifty thousand *sanzens* that he has offered to his students.

Roshi used to tell us that his teacher, Jōten Sōkō, had once told him that if you teach a thousand students and get one good student from that group, then you will have succeeded. Roshi apparently took this to heart. In *sesshin* after *sesshin* he manifested the unique form of Rinzai teaching he came to call Tathāgata (Nyorai) Zen, a teaching that is experientially grounded, philosophically dense, and singularly innovative within the Mahayana Buddhist tradition. Hinting at a secret lineage and—in the tradition of Confucius—implying that he "did not create, only transmit," Roshi developed his philosophy in a myriad of talks, including the hundreds of lectures he gave at the thirty-seven Seminars on the Sutras—annual events that began in 1977. These were all oral teachings.

Over the years during visits over tea, I would find Roshi writing in tiny Japanese characters on narrow-lined notebook paper. When I asked him what he was writing, he would reply, "Roshi's writing a book," and then place the sheet of paper on which he was writing into a cardboard box, where it joined what seemed like hundreds of others. With no sign of the manuscript for a long while, one afternoon five years ago, while having tea after *sesshin*, I asked him what had happened to his "book." Looking up with his characteristic mischievous grin, he snapped out in perfect English, "Roshi burned it!"

The words that have found their way into this volume may be all that's left of this "book"; maybe they're not. Maybe they're not even related. They were discovered in a plastic bin underneath Roshi's bed when he was hospitalized in January 2012 with what most thought would be his final illness. There are no dates on this manuscript, which was written in the same tiny characters as his "book." They were transcribed into a computer file by Myōren Yasukawa, his Inji (attendant). To ensure accuracy, she checked each character with Roshi and also consulted an earlier version of the same manuscript that contained Roshi's own detailed notes. This meticulous process took many months.

Roshi handed me the manuscript in May 2013 with the request that I translate and publish it. Realizing it was beyond my own skills, I enlisted the assistance of Michel Mohr, a professor at the University of Hawaii, whose erudite and clear translation informs this publication. Wherever there was a need for clarification regarding idiosyncratic turns of phrase or relatively obscure details of Roshi's teaching, I attempted to bring the student's touch to the translation. For the most challenging passages, I sought the advice of Victor Sōgen Hori of McGill University. Another friend and colleague, Paula Arai of Louisiana State University, working with Kai Chan, reviewed the Japanese text, as did Professor Mohr. Any mistakes that may have entered either the Japanese text or the English translation are my responsibility.

We present this book to Jōshū Rōshi on the occasion of the fifty-second anniversary of his coming to America. With Roshi no longer actively teaching, this book is the first publication of the many materials that will constitute part of the legacy of his unique form of Rinzai Zen in the Western world.

Kendō Hal Roth
July 21, 2014

Printed and bound by Coach House Press, Toronto
Limited edition Japanese binding by Don Taylor, Toronto
Text paper: Rolland Zephyr Antique Laid by Cascades, St. Jerome, Quebec
Limited edition cover paper: Canal Coffee Sisal by Papeterie Saint-Armand, Montreal
Limited edition endpapers: Kozo #14 by Matsuo Washi, Fukuoka, Japan
Trade edition cover paper: Via Jute by Mohawk Fine Papers, Cohoes, New York
English typeface: Goluska by Rod McDonald, Lake Echo, Nova Scotia
Japanese typeface: Kozuka Mincho Pro by Masahiko Kozuka, Tokyo